# Watery Worlds

# COASTS AND SEASHORES

## Jinny Johnson

W
FRANKLIN WATTS
LONDON•SYDNEY

An Appleseed Editions book

First published in 2011 by Franklin Watts
338 Euston Road, London NW1 3BH

Franklin Watts Australia
Hachette Children's Books
Level 17/207 Kent St, Sydney, NSW 2000

© 2011 Appleseed Editions

Created by Appleseed Editions Ltd,
Well House, Friars Hill, Guestling,
East Sussex TN35 4ET

Designed by Hel James
Illustrations by Graham Rosewarne
Edited by Mary-Jane Wilkins
Picture research by Su Alexander

ISBN 978-1-4451-0377-8
Dewey Classification 577.6'99

A CIP catalogue for this book is available from the British Library.

Picture credits
Contents page Tuulijumala/Shutterstock; 4 Roseanne Smith/Shutterstock; 5 Emjay Smith/
Shutterstock; 6 Sean Bolton/Alamy, 6/7 background Stephen Meese/Shutterstock, 7 Timothy Epp/
Shutterstock; 8 Bradley Allen Murrell/Shutterstock, 8/9 background Stephen Aaron Rees/Shutterstock,
9t Ekaterina Pokrovsky/Shutterstock, b R Gino Santa Maria/Shutterstock; 10 Cary Kalscheuer/
Shutterstock, 10/11 background Stephen Meese, 11 Tatiana Belova/Shutterstock;
12 Rico/Shutterstock; 13t JonMilnes/Shutterstock, b Joe Belanger/Shutterstock; 14 Cigdem Cooper/
Shutterstock, 14/15 background Tuulijumala/Shutterstock, 15t Vittorio Bruno/Shutterstock,
b Abraham Badenhorst; 16 A & S Aakjaer/Shutterstock, 16/17 background Stephen Aaron Rees/
Shutterstock, 17t Ian Scott/Shutterstock, b David Dohnal/Shutterstock; 18 Neelsky/Shutterstock,
18/19 background Stephen Meese/Shutterstock, 19t EcoPrint/Shutterstock, bl Sergey Khachatryan/
Shutterstock, br Nikita Tiunov/Shutterstock; 20 Andrea Leone/Shutterstock, 20/21 background
Tuulijumala/Shutterstock, 21t Kirsten Wahlquist/Shutterstock, b Andrea Haase/Shutterstock;
22 Nina B /Shutterstock, 22/23 background Michael Zysman/Shutterstock, 23 Rebvt/Shutterstock;
124 Vatikaki/Shutterstock; 25t Heiko Kiera/Shutterstock, b Rich Carey/Shutterstock;
26 Hugh Landsdown/Shutterstock, 26/27 background Frontpage/Shutterstock,
27t Marco Alegria/Shutterstock, b Bernhard Richter; 29 Holger W/Shutterstock;
30/31 background Tuulijumala/Shutterstock
Front cover main image Stephen Aaron Rees/Shutterstock, below left to right: Ecoprint/Shutterstock,
A & S Aakjaer/Shutterstock, JonMilnes/Shutterstock

Printed in Singapore

Franklin Watts is a division of Hachette Children's Books,
an Hachette UK company.
www.hachette.co.uk

# Contents

Life between the tides     4

Rock clingers     6

Hidden in the sand     8

Life in a rock pool     10

Seashore fish     12

Slugs, snails and octopuses     14

Coastal birds     16

Crabs, shrimp and lobsters     18

Seals and sea lions     20

Marine iguanas     22

Nesting on the beach     24

Life in a mangrove swamp     26

World oceans: Atlantic     28

Watery words     30

Index     32

# Life between the tides

The seashore is where land and water meet. Twice a day the tide goes in and out. The waves surge up sandy beaches or crash on to rocky shores.

This might seem a difficult place for animals to live. At some times of day they are exposed to the wind and sun, and at other times they are underwater.

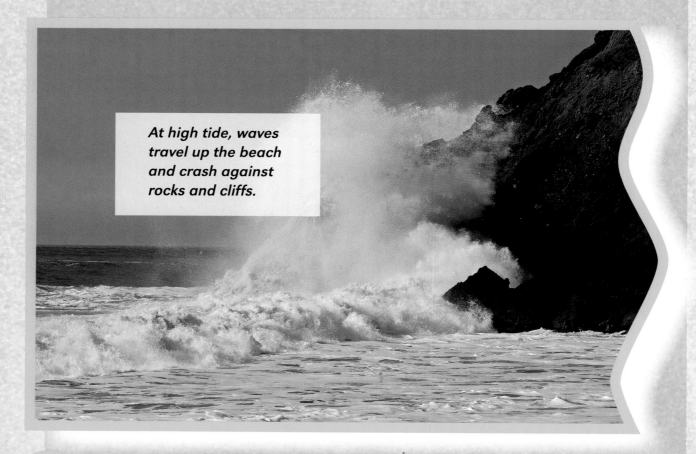

At high tide, waves travel up the beach and crash against rocks and cliffs.

In fact, the seashore is bursting with life, both in the shallow water close to the land and on the shore itself. Some seashore creatures survive because they have hard shells to protect them; others live in burrows or shelter among seaweeds.

**Amazing!**

Almost all (about 90 per cent) of sea creatures live in coastal areas.

*At low tide, much of the beach is open to the sun and wind. Some creatures hide in pools. Others close their shells to protect themselves.*

**Guess what?**
The Moon controls the tides on Earth. It pulls the water in the oceans towards it by a force called gravity.

# Rock clingers

Not all sea creatures swim and dive. Some spend nearly all their time in one place, often on rocks on the seashore. Many have special ways of clinging to their home so they don't get washed away as the tide goes in and out.

Limpets, barnacles and mussels start life as tiny creatures that float in the sea as they grow. When they are fully grown, they settle on a rock or other surface. Barnacles and mussels do not move again. Limpets do move around feeding on **algae**, a kind of seaweed, but only when the rocks are wet or covered by the tide.

*A limpet clings to surfaces with a part of its body called its foot, which acts like a sucker to keep it in place. Some limpets make their home on boats or even whales!*

Limpets leave a sticky trail when they move around so they can always find their way back to the same spot.

**Amazing!**

## Guess what?

Do you know how a barnacle feeds? When it is covered by water at high tide, a barnacle opens its shell at the top and sticks out its feathery arms. It uses these to gather tiny bits of food from the water.

*Sticky threads hold a mussel on to its rocky home and help it stay put through the roughest tides.*

# Hidden in the sand

Seabirds patrol the beach and look for clams and other animals that shelter in the seaweed.

The sand on a sandy shore is made by the waves pounding on bits of rock and shell over many years. A sandy beach may look very empty, with few places for creatures to live. In fact, there are many animals, but most of them live below the surface.

Lots of lugworms live on sandy beaches. They live in burrows shaped like tubes. Look out for little dips in the sand – a sure sign of a lugworm burrow. Different kinds of clam make burrows too.

A razor clam can dig fast. It can bury itself in less than seven seconds when it is in danger.

**Amazing!**

*Look out for lugworm burrows like these. Each burrow has a little pile of waste next to it.*

Crabs sometimes scuttle across the beach and then burrow under the sand. Little beach hoppers or beach fleas hide in the sand during the day. They come out at night to feed on anything washed up by the tide.

*Crabs have ten legs. They swim well and can walk on the seabed.*

## WATCH OUT!

We all love sandy beaches but we can damage them easily. Lots of people walking around can disturb burrows and flatten the sand so it becomes hard and compact. Cars and beach buggies do more serious harm. Litter on the beach may hurt creatures, which may try to eat it, so always take your rubbish home.

# Life in a rock pool

When the tide goes out, some creatures stay behind in little pools left in dips and hollows in the rocks. The pool has to be quite deep so it doesn't dry up on a hot day and have plenty of hiding places for snails, crabs and prawns.

Look out for sea anemones in rock pools. They look more like flowers than animals, but they are **predators** and catch other animals to eat. A sea anemone catches its **prey** with its stinging **tentacles** and then pulls it into its mouth. It spends most of its life fixed to one place by a sucking disc at the end of its body.

*Starfish, sea urchins and sea anemones are some of the creatures living in this rock pool.*

## Guess what?

Clownfish can live around a sea anemone without being harmed by its stinging tentacles and this is good for both animals. The fish is safe from other predators as it cleans scraps and algae off the anemone. In return, the anemone doesn't harm the fish.

Most sea anemones measure just a few centimetres across, but the largest grows up to 1.5 metres.

**Amazing!**

The sea anemone can pull all its tentacles inside its body when it is in danger from an attacker.

# Seashore fish

Lots of fish live in the shallow waters just off the seashore. Among them are wrasse, seahorses, blennies and gobies – any of them might swim round your feet as you splash in the sea.

Gobies and blennies also live in rock pools. The fins on a goby's belly are joined together to make a kind of sucking disc. This helps the fish cling to the rock so it is not swept away by crashing waves.

*This goby is clinging to a rock with the help of the special fins on its belly.*

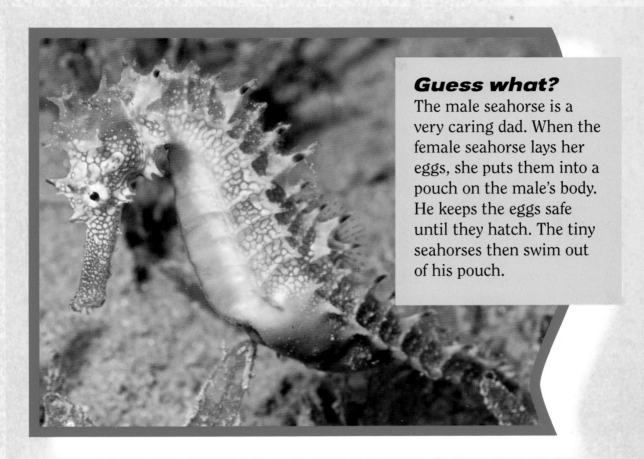

### Guess what?

The male seahorse is a very caring dad. When the female seahorse lays her eggs, she puts them into a pouch on the male's body. He keeps the eggs safe until they hatch. The tiny seahorses then swim out of his pouch.

## Amazing!

Some wrasse are also known as cleaner fish. They take away dead skin, scales and little creatures called parasites from larger fish. Some even swim into the mouth of larger fish to clean rubbish from their teeth.

# Slugs, snails and octopuses

Snails, sea slugs and octopuses look different from each other, but they all belong to the same group of creatures, called **molluscs**. Periwinkles are sea snails; you can see them on rocks and in rock pools on every beach.

Sea slugs are snails without a shell and they are more brightly coloured than land slugs. Sea slugs live in all parts of the ocean, but a lot of them live in coastal waters. They hunt other creatures, such as anemones, **sponges** and even other sea slugs.

Some sea slugs change colour depending on what they eat. If a sea slug eats a red sponge it turns red.

**Amazing!**

14

An octopus is much larger than a sea slug. It has a pouch-like body and eight arms, which are lined with suckers. Octopuses often hide under rocks in shallow water close to the shore, watching out for prey such as crabs and clams.

### Guess what?

An octopus likes to stay hidden – from its enemies as well as from prey it is sneaking up on. It can change the colour and pattern of its skin almost instantly to match its surroundings, making it very hard to see.

# Coastal birds

Gannets, pelicans and other coastal birds do not live in the sea. They spend their lives on the shore and find their food in the water. They eat mainly fish and squid and have their own ways of catching food.

The gannet flies high over the water, looking out for any sign of fish. If it sees one, the gannet dives down into the sea with its wings held back neatly to **streamline** its body.

*A gannet snatches fish from the sea with its dagger-like beak.*

**Amazing!**

A gannet can dive into the water at up to 100 kilometres per hour.

## WATCH OUT!

Oil spills and other **pollution** can harm shore birds. Oil damages the birds' feathers and other chemicals make them ill. The birds may also swallow cigarette ends, plastic bags and other litter, which can kill them.

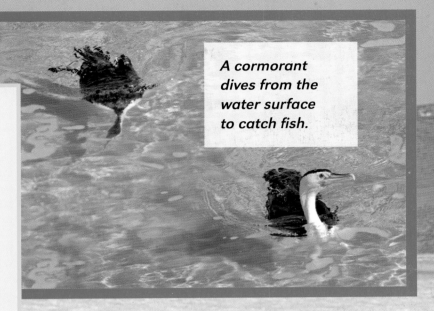

*A cormorant dives from the water surface to catch fish.*

Cormorants chase their prey very fast underwater and go back to the surface to eat their catch. Oystercatchers look for food on the shoreline. They pick up shellfish such as oysters and clams with their long beaks.

*An oystercatcher picks up a mussel to eat the soft flesh inside the shell.*

# Crabs, shrimp and lobsters

These creatures are part of a group of animals called **crustaceans**. Most of them live in the sea. A crustacean has a shell which protects its soft body. It also has two sets of feelers, or **antennae**, and three pairs of mouthparts, as well as lots of legs.

Lobsters and crabs are large crustaceans with strong shells and big pincers. They use these to break open the shells of their prey. They have five pairs of legs and can scuttle over rocks and the seabed as well as swim. Shrimps have much lighter shells and long antennae that help them find tiny bits of food in the water.

A lobster can live as long as 50 years and keeps growing all through its life.

**Amazing!**

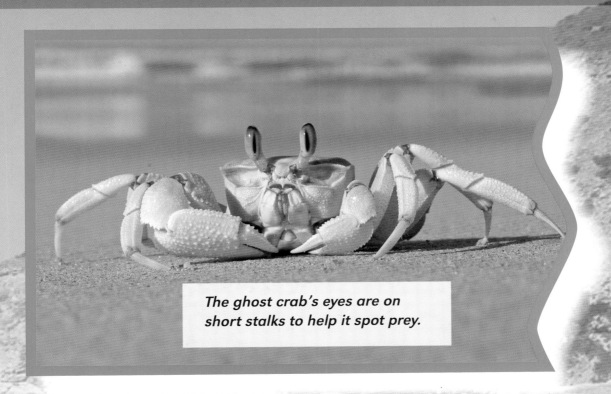

*The ghost crab's eyes are on short stalks to help it spot prey.*

### Guess what?

A hermit crab doesn't have a hard shell like other crabs. It lives in a shell left by another creature, such as a periwinkle or other snail. As the crab grows bigger, it has to swap its shell for a larger one.

*The striped cleaner shrimp eats tiny creatures and dead skin off other animals.*

# Seals and sea lions

These animals live in the sea, but they are not fish. They are **mammals**, like cats, dogs and monkeys. Although they live in the sea they cannot breathe in water and they have to come to the surface to take a breath of air.

Seals and sea lions have flippers instead of legs and these help them swim. Their bodies are covered with fur and a thick layer of fat called **blubber**, which keeps them warm in the coldest sea. These animals spend most of their time in the water. They do come on to land sometimes to lie on rocks in the sun and to **mate** and give birth to their young.

## Amazing!

If a sea lion is feeling chilly on a sunny day, it sticks a flipper out of the water to soak up some heat from the sun.

## Guess what?

The sea otter, another sea-living mammal, has learned how to use a tool to open shellfish. When a sea otter finds a clam, it also picks up a rock. It then floats on its back and bangs the clam with the rock until the shell breaks open.

Female Australian sea lions give birth to just one pup at a time. The mum feeds and cares for her pup for up to a year.

# Marine iguanas

These giant iguanas are the only lizards that live in the sea. Their home is the rocky shores of the Galapagos Islands, off the coast of South America, and they grow to 1.5 metres long.

The marine iguana looks fierce, but it feeds on algae, a type of seaweed. It scrapes its food off rocks with its small sharp teeth. It swims and dives well and can stay underwater for up to an hour. When it comes out of the cold water, it **basks** on the rocks on the shore to warm itself up.

**Amazing!**

A marine iguana swallows lots of salt water, but it has special glands that help it get rid of salt from its body. When the iguana sneezes, a spray of salt comes out.

## WATCH OUT!

Marine iguanas were once very safe on their islands. Then people brought cats, rats and dogs to the islands. These eat the iguana's eggs and even the animals themselves. The number of iguanas has gone down and they need to be protected from these other animals to survive.

*Salt from the iguana's sneezes lands on its head and looks like a little white hat.*

# Nesting on the beach

Some of the biggest of all turtles live in the sea. A turtle has a shell to protect its body, like a land tortoise, but it has long flippers instead of legs. There are seven different kinds of sea turtle.

Turtles find their food in the water and spend nearly all their lives in the sea. Females come to land to lay their eggs. They swim to nesting beaches, often making a very long journey. The turtle then drags herself up on to land, digs a pit and lays her eggs.

*A turtle covers her clutch of eggs with sand to hide them from hungry predators.*

*Birds eat many baby turtles before they get to the sea.*

She goes back to the sea, leaving her eggs to stay warm in the pit. When the young hatch out from the eggs they have to make their way out of the nest and down to the sea.

## WATCH OUT!

All sea turtles are now rare and some are in danger of disappearing forever. Many are killed by accident in fishing nets and people also catch turtles to eat and for their shells. Turtles are also harmed by pollution – many choke on plastic bags, which they try to eat, thinking they are jellyfish.

*A green turtle beating its flippers like wings as it swims.*

### Amazing!

The biggest sea turtle is the leatherback. It weighs more than three grown-up people and eats mainly jellyfish.

# Life in a mangrove swamp

Mangrove swamps are a very special kind of seashore world on some tropical coasts. Mangrove trees can live with their roots in salt water, unlike other trees.

Fiddler crabs and many kinds of fish, such as mudskippers and archerfish, shelter among the roots of mangrove trees. Some feed on the leaves and bits of bark that fall from the trees. Egrets, anhingas and other fish-eating birds visit the mangroves to find food. Biggest of all mangrove creatures are the saltwater crocodiles, which live in swamps in South-East Asia and northern Australia.

### Guess what?
The mudskipper fish can move around out of water for a short time. At low tide it hops along over the mud with the help of its fins and some mudskippers can even climb trees.

*The male fiddler crab has an extra-large claw. He uses this to tell females he is ready to mate, not for feeding.*

**Amazing!**

Saltwater crocodiles are the largest crocodiles in the world and the most dangerous. The biggest measure up to 7 metres – longer than three people lying head to toe.

# World oceans: Atlantic

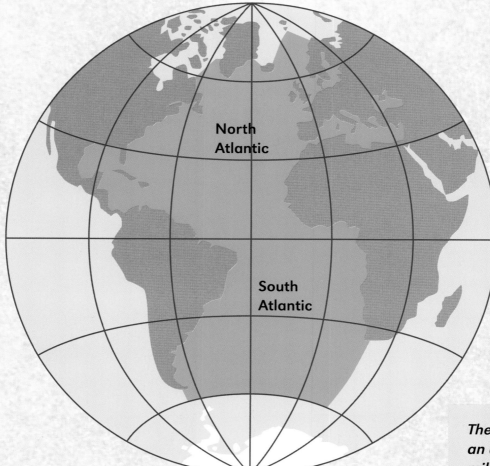

North
Atlantic

South
Atlantic

The Atlantic is the second largest ocean in the world. It covers one fifth of the Earth's surface. The ocean lies between North and South America to the west and Europe and Africa in the east. It includes the Caribbean Sea, the Mediterranean, the North Sea and the Black Sea. It reaches to the Arctic Ocean in the north and the Southern Ocean in the south.

*The Atlantic covers an area of 76,762 million sq km. That's more than six times bigger than the area of the United States.*

# Atlantic facts

The shortest Atlantic crossing is between Senegal in Africa and north-eastern Brazil in South America.

The average depth of the Atlantic Ocean is 3,660 metres. If you put the seven tallest buildings in the world into the sea, one on top of the other, the top one would only just peek above the surface.

The deepest point of the Atlantic is the Puerto Rico Trench, which is an amazing 8,530 metres deep. Even Mount Everest, the world's highest mountain, would almost disappear in that.

Many of the world's largest rivers flow into the Atlantic, including the Mississippi, the Congo and the Amazon.

*This is a modern replica of the* Santa Maria. *It was the largest of the three ships on Christopher Columbus's first voyage across the Atlantic in 1492.*

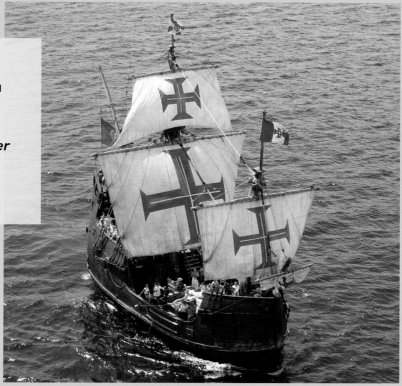

# Watery words

**algae**
A type of simple green plant that lives in water.

**antennae**
A pair of long thin body parts on the head of an animal such as a shrimp. Antennae help animals to sense things around them.

**bask**
To lie in the sun or other warmth.

**blubber**
A layer of fat covering the body of a marine mammal such as a seal or a whale. The fat helps to keep the animal warm.

**crustacean**
One of a group of animals that includes crabs, lobsters and shrimp. Most have a tough outer shell.

**gland**
A part of an animal's body that makes substances or does particular things.

**mammal**
A warm-blooded animal that feeds its babies with milk from its own body. Land mammals have four legs but sea-living mammals, such as whales and seals, have flippers instead.

**mate**
Male and female animals pair up, or mate, to produce young. An animal's partner is its mate.

**mollusc**
One of a group of animals that includes clams, mussels and octopuses. Most have a hard shell.

**parasites**
Small creatures that live on or in the bodies of larger animals.

**pollution**
The introduction of things that damage the natural world, such as litter and oil.

**predator**
An animal that hunts and kills other animals to eat.

**prey**
An animal hunted and eaten by another animal.

**sponge**
A very simple animal that lives in water.

**streamline**
To make a neat shape that moves easily through air or water.

**tentacles**
A long body part, usually around the mouth, used for holding prey or food.

# Index

algae 6, 11, 22, 30
antennae 18, 30

barnacles 6, 7
beach hoppers 9
blennies 12
blubber 20, 30

clams 8, 15, 17, 21
clownfish 11
cormorants 17
crabs 9, 10, 15, 18,
  19, 26, 27
crocodiles 26, 27
crustaceans 18, 30

eggs 13, 23, 24, 25

fins 12, 26
flippers 20, 24, 25

gannets 16
gobies 12

iguanas 22-23

limpets 6
litter 9, 17
lobsters 18
lugworms 8, 9

molluscs 14, 31
mudskippers 26
mussels 6, 7, 17

octopuses 14, 15
oystercatchers 17

parasites 13, 31
periwinkles 14, 19
pollution 17, 25, 31
predators 10, 11, 24,
  31
prey 10, 15, 17, 18,
  19, 31

rock pools 5, 10-11,
  12, 14

sea anemones 10, 11,
  14
sea lions 20, 21

sea otters 21
sea slugs 14
sea urchins 10
seahorses 12, 13
seals 20
seaweeds 5, 6, 8, 22
shells 5, 7, 8, 14, 17,
  18, 19, 21, 24, 25
shrimp 18, 19
snails 10, 14, 19
sponges 14, 31
starfish 10

tentacles 10, 11, 31
turtles 24-25

wrasse 12, 13